I0504208

Multiple Sources of Income

What you need to know

TOMY SHAW

DEDICATION

This book is a dedication to all the people who suffer with their finances, and my goal is to help people take control over their finances and for them to learn how to invest and create wealth.

CONTENTS

ACKNOWLEDGMENTS

I want to acknowledge my family for having the patience for me to write this book, I had to take a lot of time away from them, and sometimes I was there, but I was thinking about the book.

1 STARTING

How would you feel if money kept coming in, occasionally, you receive a check of a hundred dollars here, hundred dollars there? Well, it's possible, once you understand the sources of income, you will realize that money does not have the same value, depending on either of its origin, earned income, is taxed at the highest, then capital gains are taxed at different levels.

The rich can work for money, but one thing that they do differently is they make their money work for them. There have multiple ways to make money and to grow it. I have always been interested in this area of my life, making money work for me, it began with small amounts, but I could not get my head around the fact that money could work for me, I remember receiving my first monthly interest check, it was 3.57$, I was so happy, since I did not have to work for that money, it was free money. At the time, I did not have any concepts of the effect of inflation or even the term inflation.

This is where my story begins, and now, only ten years later, making enough money per month to cover all of my monthly expenses, one could say that I am retired, of course, I will not retire, but it could be a choice, I simply believe that being productive bring me happiness. I tried staying at home for one year, and I was not feeling fulfilled, and this is where my journey of trying many sources of income to see what worked and what I failed badly.

I have invested in jewelry, stocks, mutual funds, ETFs, bonds, blogs, selling on Amazon, investing in real estate, and tax liens. I have even tried affiliate marketing. Through the next pages, I will show my experiences in all those avenues to help the reader understand all the roads so that he can take the best path for each personality.

Of course, all these methods, capital will be needed, either through internal financing or directly from the money that you have saved. If you do not value and protect your cash, multiple sources of income might not be possible or take longer. I was saving seventy percent of my salary, and this gave me the ability to be free under ten years.

Passive income also provides the tool necessary to use the power of compounding. It gives the ability to every dollar to grow, just like a tree, learning to think in nonlinear fashion can be hard at first, but when it is understood, you will not see money in the same way, you will see every dollar as a seed that can grow into millions. When I look at the evolution of my equity, assets, and liabilities, they have grown in the shape of a hockey stick, they have all compounded and kept increasing very quickly, at first it was slow but when the momentum started to kick in, I could not believe the wealth that I had acquired over the years and you do the same thing as I state in this book, I think that you can receive the same results.

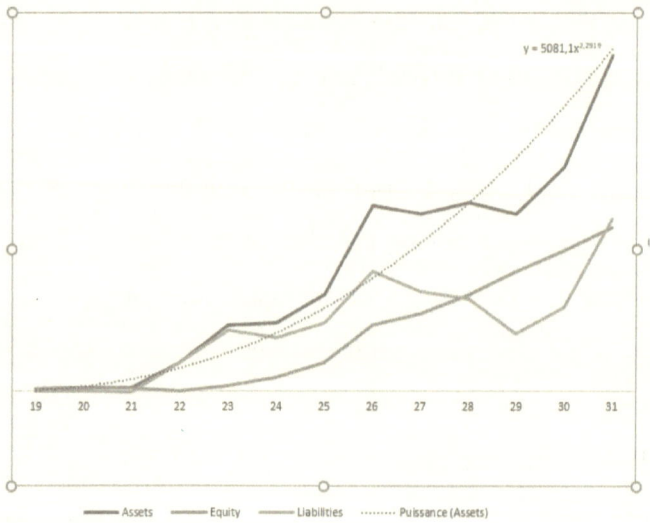

$y = 5081.1x^{2.2919}$

It is my wealth has grown over the years, as we can see my wealth is increasing at an exponential way, we can also notice that when I acquire significant assets with debt, that my equity seems to grow quicker in the years to come. The years that I had paid a lot of debt, my capital started to look like a straight line. I must note that most of those assets are in real estate.

Here is an example of how compound interest can make a big difference in the long run of two people investing at different ages ten thousand dollars at 7 percent interest, if Roger fund at the age of twenty and say Steven started at the age of thirty, at the age of 66, Rogers will have amassed 210 024.52$, compared to Steven 76 122.56. That is almost three times as much. Therefore, it is imperative to start investing young.

Age	Roger	Age	Roger	Steven	Age	Roger	Steven
		35	27 590,32 $	10 000,00 $	51	76 122,55 $	27 590,32 $
20	10 000,00 $	36	29 521,64 $	10 700,00 $	52	81 451,13 $	29 521,64 $
21	10 700,00 $	37	31 588,15 $	11 449,00 $	53	87 152,71 $	31 588,16 $
22	11 449,00 $	38	33 799,32 $	12 250,43 $	54	93 253,40 $	33 799,33 $
23	12 250,43 $	39	36 165,28 $	13 107,96 $	55	99 781,13 $	36 165,28 $
24	13 107,96 $	40	38 696,84 $	14 025,52 $	56	106 765,81 $	38 696,85 $
25	14 025,52 $	41	41 405,62 $	15 007,30 $	57	114 239,42 $	41 405,63 $
26	15 007,30 $	42	44 304,02 $	16 057,81 $	58	122 236,18 $	44 304,02 $
27	16 057,81 $	43	47 405,30 $	17 181,86 $	59	130 792,71 $	47 405,31 $
28	17 181,86 $	44	50 723,67 $	18 384,59 $	60	139 948,20 $	50 723,68 $
29	18 384,59 $	45	54 274,33 $	19 671,51 $	61	149 744,58 $	54 274,34 $
30	19 671,51 $	46	58 073,53 $	21 048,52 $	62	160 226,70 $	58 073,54 $
31	21 048,52 $	47	62 138,68 $	22 521,92 $	63	171 442,57 $	62 138,69 $
32	22 521,92 $	48	66 488,38 $	24 098,45 $	64	183 443,55 $	66 488,39 $
33	24 098,45 $	49	71 142,57 $	25 785,34 $	65	196 284,59 $	71 142,58 $
34	25 785,34 $	50	76 122,55 $	27 590,32 $	66	210 024,52 $	76 122,56 $

This example becomes even more pronounced when contributing every year 10 000$, and interest rates are higher, and this higher return can be achieved by using leverage, in real estate, it is common to make twenty percent on the capital invested. Here is the same example as the last figure but compounded at ten percent per year.

Age	Roger	Age	Roger	Steven	Age	Roger	Steven
		35	40 633,23 $	10 000,00 $	51	186 708,60 $	45 949,73 $
20	10 000,00 $	36	44 696,56 $	11 000,00 $	52	205 379,46 $	50 544,70 $
21	11 000,00 $	37	49 166,21 $	12 100,00 $	53	225 917,41 $	55 599,17 $
22	12 100,00 $	38	54 082,83 $	13 310,00 $	54	248 509,15 $	61 159,09 $
23	13 310,00 $	39	59 491,12 $	14 641,00 $	55	273 360,07 $	67 275,00 $
24	14 641,00 $	40	65 440,23 $	16 105,10 $	56	300 696,07 $	74 002,50 $
25	16 105,10 $	41	71 984,25 $	17 715,61 $	57	330 765,68 $	81 402,75 $
26	17 715,61 $	42	79 182,67 $	19 487,17 $	58	363 842,25 $	89 543,02 $
27	19 487,17 $	43	87 100,94 $	21 435,89 $	59	400 226,47 $	98 497,33 $
28	21 435,89 $	44	95 811,04 $	23 579,48 $	60	440 249,12 $	108 347,06 $
29	23 579,48 $	45	105 392,14 $	25 937,42 $	61	484 274,03 $	119 181,77 $
30	25 937,42 $	46	115 931,35 $	28 531,17 $	62	532 701,44 $	131 099,94 $
31	28 531,17 $	47	127 524,49 $	31 384,28 $	63	585 971,58 $	144 209,94 $
32	31 384,28 $	48	140 276,94 $	34 522,71 $	64	644 568,74 $	158 630,93 $
33	34 522,71 $	49	154 304,63 $	37 974,98 $	65	709 025,61 $	174 494,02 $
34	37 974,98 $	50	169 735,09 $	41 772,48 $	66	779 928,18 $	191 943,42 $

As we can see, the amount start spread out by a lot more, almost five times as Steven. The younger you can save and invest will make a big difference in the long run. Of course, this example does not include income taxes and inflation. It is to be noted that these two elements will harm the real value that you have acquired over the years.

The spread would get even higher if we were to add a few years to the example. The amount that is invested at the beginning, the interest that the compounds get inserted, payments that is contributed per year and the number of years that the amount are invested.

It led me to the importance of managing and tracking your income and expenses if you are not accountable to the money that you are earning right now, more money will equate to the same results. Managing is the first essential step to acquiring wealth. Here are some sites that can help;

·   Learn Vest;

·   Mint;

·   The Birdy;

·   Daily Worth;

·   NerdWallet;

Once we know how much you are earning and spending per month, we can find out how much is your surplus/deficit. You must make sure that all expenses are included in your expense column.

If the results are negative, then something will need to be done, either you cut down on some expenses that are not necessary or that you take on another part-time job to help the ability to save some money. I know that this step is not pleasing to here, but in the long run, the sacrifice will be worth it. It is also about building the discipline necessary to build wealth, and it is a crucial step in the process of becoming wealthy. There is no way around it.

Now we must make monthly goals and the ways to achieve this is by making daily goals. Say, you would like to save 300$ a month, divide that number by 30, and this gives you a regular purpose of ten dollars a day. By giving yourself daily goals, this gives you the ability to achieve your goals daily, and they also become straightforward to achieve. I do this with all my goals. I break them into daily goals and track them daily. It makes me accountable for my action if I do not achieve my daily goal, I know, that on the next day, I might have to double my efforts. It is essential not to try a rationalize your results.

Now that we have started saving some money, what do we do with it? Well, you can take your skill and offer it on the sides or start investing in other avenues of income, what I look like to mention, there is a time for sowing and a time for reaping. It took me a long time to understand this statement, I would compare it to the seasons of the year, but in passive income or other streams of income, the winter and spring can take up to four years before the results start to compound.

I am mentioning it for the simple fact that when you want to explore other avenues of income, you should keep your current employment to give you the ability to keep living and taking some surplus to help grow your additional streams of income. It will also give you the ability to borrow at lower rates. Again, helping you to grow.

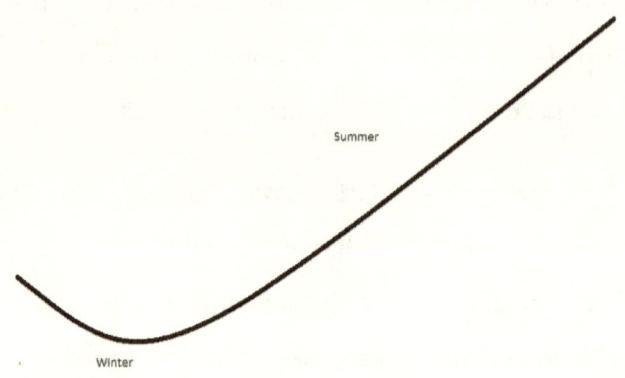

It leads to saving money, and it is imperative to save money, to invest, the more you save, the faster your wealth will grow short term and especially in the long run. To become a millionaire in under ten years at ten percent interest, you must invest 4 881.74 per month. It might seem like a lot, but when you acquire some assets with leverage, the cumulative amount multiplies.

If you would of ask me that I would have become a millionaire in under ten years, I would not have believed it, what I wanted at eighteen years, was to get financial freedom. I did not like what I was doing, and my goal was to cut the middle, buy a house and expensive car.

The reason I wanted to achieve my goal so badly was because I had some coworkers that was still working at a job that they didn't like and still had money problems. I did not want to become that person.

To help understand the value of your interest saved on your house and expenses that you do, I would recommend that you download these two applications, the reason them is because I use them;

1. Fncalculator.com
2. Karl's Mortgage Calculator

The first application help to understand the value of future money and the second calculator helps to know how much the payments will be on the house that you buy, the impact on the mortgage loan when you make lump-sum payments.

I will show how my wealth has evolved over the years and where it came from, well, let's dive in.

2 REAL ESTATE

Real estate has been very successful for me, I have made most of the wealth through this vehicle, was it the easiest? No, the money and wealth that I have received from this avenue was stressful and a lot of work.

The first property that I bought was in 2010, it was a single-family home, and we had purchased that home to live in. A few months had passed, and we decided that if we want to invest in real estate, that we should try to rent some rooms to see if we could manage tenants. We rented out four bedrooms, all that money gave us the ability to live at home for free, and we were even making some cashflow. The house was making about eleven hundred a month, and we had expenses of a thousand per month.

The powerful thing about this avenue is that all the money that was made, we didn't have to pay taxes since we could use depreciation and the house had a lot of expenses, that brought down the profits of the house. It was magical.

Remember, taxes are paid on the profits of the property, imagine, making money in real estate gives you the ability to spend before any taxes are paid to the government, there is a lot of purchasing power for this income.

Now, the next deal, it was a fourplex, and we had bought this property in 2011, only eight months after we had bought our first home. We had a bought this fourplex for a 184 000$, after paying all the expenses and mortgage, it was clearing four hundred dollars a month. It was an excellent property with great tenants. There were not a lot of work that needs to be done, and the location was great. We felt that we were protected in real estate, everything we did worked.

The next step that we decided to do was to pay our home, every month, we would live on one salary, and we would take the other to pay off our home mortgage, in 2013, only two years and a half after that we had bought home, it was paid for. It was a fantastic feeling to me, it was my life goal, and it seemed so big that we had already achieved it made me feel very rich and grateful. The hard work had paid off.

Now, in 2013, we decided to invest in our local tax liens certificates, it was something that we had read, but we know no one that was investing in this avenue. After searching many properties, we had bought a house, it was 150K, but we had only paid 40K, this meant that we would make 110K if we kept the home. Buying certificates, the owner had one year to rebuy the property, and he needs to pay the amount that you have paid plus a ten percent fee, which the owner did. He had bought the property four months after that we had, this gave us a capital gain of four thousand dollars, this was great, we only had put a couple of hours work, it was a high return.

In 2014, we had bought a four-plex, a six-plex and another tax lien. It was a big year, the four-plex, we had purchased the property 30k undervalue, the six-plex, we had bought a bargain also, and the tax liens, we had invested 50K. Now we had fourteen tenants to handle, and I could feel that it was starting to be a lot, I was managing the property, doing the bookkeeping and maintenance on the farms.

I knew we had to find a manager, and a friend had recommended it to his manager. There were a lot of free time that was liberated by doing this. He would rent, do the paperwork to get bad tenants out, and he would find contractors and negotiate the price to maintain the property.

This free time gave me the ability to learn how to invest in stocks. I had no experience and did not know to find companies or trade them — more on this subject later in the book.

2018, we had bought another four-plex plus two other tax liens. Great year, now my real estate business is still growing, and it has given me the ability to become financially free. Would I recommend real estate, yes, I would, but I know that real estate is not for everyone, profession usually don't make it this area, since, their money earned is just too great to see the long-run potential in real estate.

I started with ten thousand dollars in real estate, and now I have a portfolio of above 1.5 million dollars' worth of asset, just to put this in perspective, if it increases only of 5% in one year, this give me 75 000$ of net worth value. I am not even taking into consideration the income coming in.

Let's look at one aspect of why real estate is so powerful. First scenario, say you have a person that is making 50K a year, and that person saves ten percent per year with an increase of 3% per of salary. This person will have accumulated from the age of 20 – 54 years approximately 320 000$

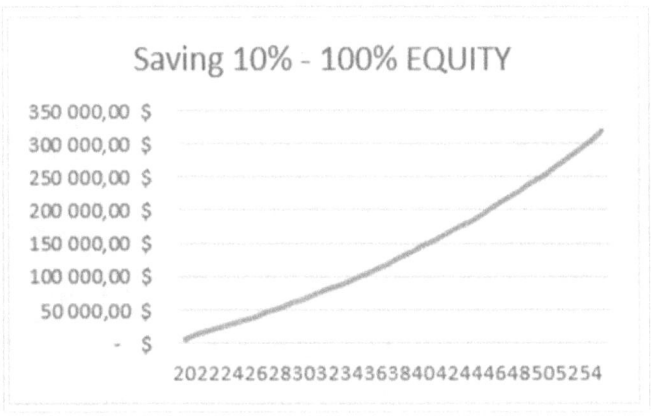

In the last example, the assets will total the net worth of the individual. Let's look at the same case, but with leverage of five times. It means that for everyone dollars of equity, you take on four dollars of debt. For this process to work, you must make sure that the investment cash flows, and it only works when you   acquire   assets   that   generate   income.

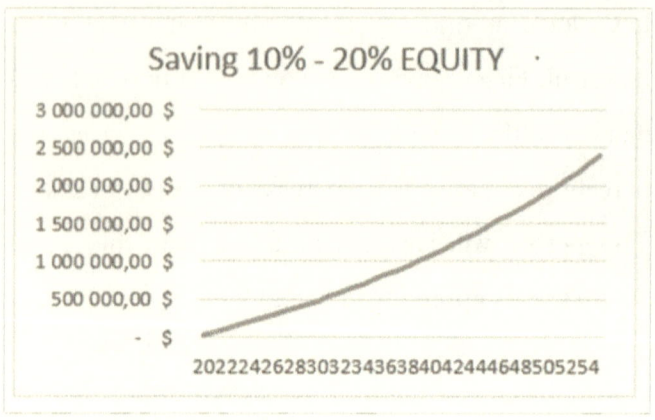

Instead of having 320K, you now have accumulated 1.6 million of assets. In the last example, it does not even include the concept of the returns of the assets. Let's look at the case in more depth by adding the profits of the assets. On average, we can conclude a 7% return on assets, including the revenues and appreciation of the assets.

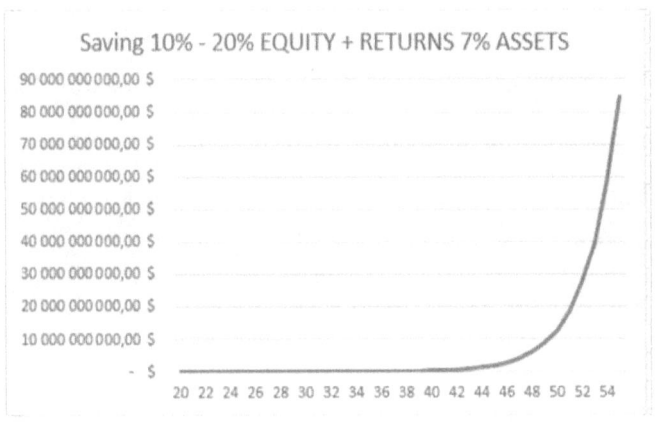

It is a hypothetical example, and if you could always invest your equity into five times the value of your capital, you would need to find deals and reinvest a hundred percent of all your returns back into the business, now this number multiplies, thanks to compound interest and the power of leverage. The number grows into the billions.

The last example shows why structuring your business, or real estate will help to grow you're at multiple times the amount that you could have saved initially, we went from 320K to billions in just a matter of time. This is why debt makes the rich more productive, I hear middle-class people saying sometimes, I would not like to pay that interest, since I have no liability I am rich, when I understand that it makes me want to explain to them why their thinking is default thinking, they do not know how wealth is created, but in the last examples hopefully will have awoke a spark in your mind.

If you would like to have more information on how to value real estate, finance it, and manage, I have a book dedicated a hundred percent to the topic. Millionaire Real Estate Investing Secrets.

3 STOCKS, MUTUAL FUNDS AND ETF'S

Stocks are a volatile market, especially if you go into penny stocks, to be called a penny stock, the value of the capital need to be lower than five dollars, yes, you can become productive quickly, but it is a little like gambling at these levels. I have always been a very secure guy in life, but in this area, I am a gambler, I am unable to think long term.

Don't get me wrong, buying index funds and investing for the long run has strong performance history. Merely buying the S&P 500 or the TSX 60 will beat inflation anytime.

I started out investing in a mutual fund, the story started in 2014, I investing in large fidelity caps, which in one year, I had made approximately twelve percent return, pretty good performance for a beginner, what I would do, is that I would screen the best performing mutual funds for a ten year period and bought the first ones in line, don't need to be rocket scientist to understand this method.

I had sold the mutual fund in 2015 since there were a lot of fees that I knew, in the long run, would hurt my portfolio. In 2015, crude oil started to fall, so I decided to invest in oil stocks, what a bad mistake that was, I decided to go all-in, in one sector. I had caught the falling knife, and my portfolio went from 150K to 40K in just under four months, I felt very depressed and angry at myself I could not believe that I had lost all that money. My wife could not believe it either.

The stock that I had bought was highly correlated with the price of crude oil, and the company was a Canadian company called Trans Globe Energy Corporation, TGL, for short.

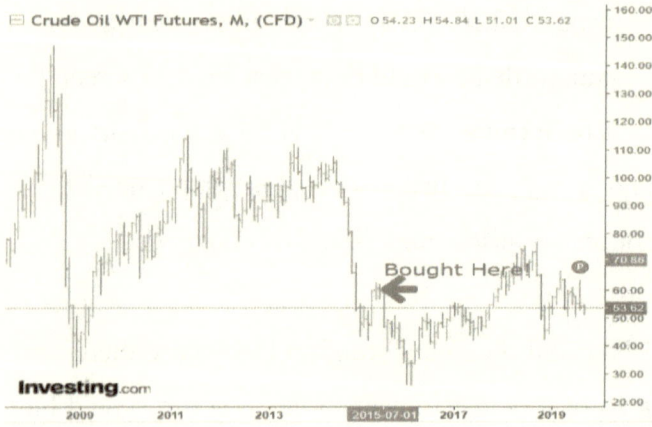

I bought the stock at around 5.40, then it went down hard, sold at the bottom. There is a saying in the market, buy low sell high, well I bought high and sold low, this was the first time in my career that I had failed badly. I could not believe that this had happened to me. I always thought that I was smarter than the average. Well, this event brought me down to earth.

I had analyzed the markets, and I was anticipating that the oil price would go higher, but they did not. I decided to keep searching, and I was sure that I could turn my situation around. After reading many books about investing in stocks, I've just finished reading, and superstocks insider buy, this book motivated me to keep going. Now I am searching for a stock that fits the criteria of the book and found a company, Chesapeake Energy, bought some shares, in one week, I had made 40K, I could not believe it, me and wife went to restaurant, and we enjoyed ourselves.

I was sure that I had found the holy grail, I started thinking about buying a home in Mexico, traveling the world, and saying to my wife that she should quit her job. I had a feeling that I had never felt before, euphoria, I hate this emotion, it's a high that does not want to go, even if you are tired, it keeps you awake, and you have a hard time believing what just happened.

As you can see, the stock kept going higher and higher, so what did I do, well I kept buying more. The more the price went up, the higher my average price went. As time went on, the markets had a pullback, which again I had lost my gains. I could not believe it; I had returned to my 40k mark. Now I was even more depressed, and I did not want to see anyone.

After a couple of months went by, I started to feel the courage to keep trying when life hit you, it takes a lot of will power to get back up. I kept searching for businesses that could increase in value and that the risk was reduced by buying at the right time. In luck, I found CLF.

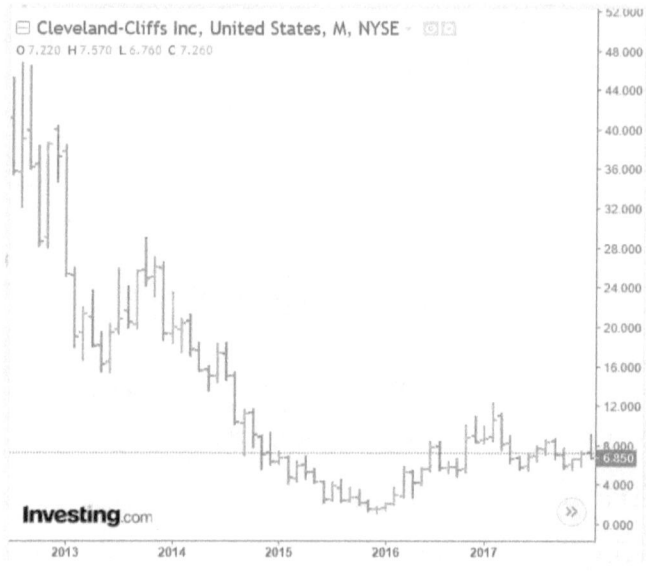

I had bought the stock at 3.26, this stock made me mad, it went up, and then it went down, I could see My portfolio goes from 40k to 120k to 60k to 120k. I sold the stock in 2018, which finally I had a collection of 120K, I decided to go all-in, CIFS, a Chinese banking company, I was following Donald Trump and the China and US trade deal, I was sure the deal would have been done, but it didn't, the stock went from 3.30$ a share to 1$, again my portfolio went down to almost 30K, how did I feel this time, well I was used to it, it did not hurt me this time, because I knew what I was getting myself into. If the stock would of went up, I was calculating that the stock could have smoothly went to 30$ a share. It would have made me a portfolio of a million dollars in stocks.

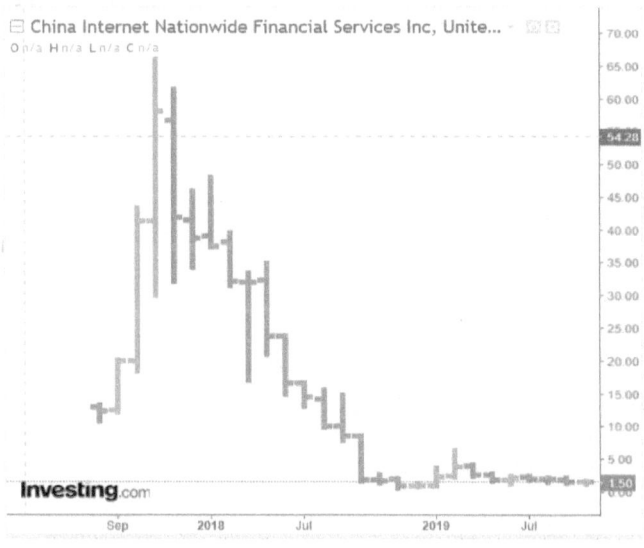

I have sold some of my position to put in CHK, thinking that the market will turn around and oil stocks might rally.

Now as the time I am writing this book, what are the mistakes that I have made, well number one, is not diversifying, well you invest diversification will reduce no systemic risk. The second big mistake that I have made was that I did not respect the markets. I did not think that it would do everything in it will do not give me easy money.

Even though all the mistakes that I have made, I still believe that it is possible to make money in the stock market.

Now the first thing that you need to invest in the financial market is a brokerage account, and I use Bank of Montreal line of action. My strategy was to buy and hold stocks for the long run, but they are many types of brokerage for the kind of investor that you will decide to become.

Here is some example of accounts;
- Interactive brokers

- Quest trade
- BMO Line of action
- Disnate
- Ninja trader
- Wealth simple

They all have pros and cons, but I have a friend that says interactive brokers is high on his list, he has a Chartered Financial Analysis, I take everything he says to heart.

Once you have set up your brokerage account, now it is time to select and learn about some stocks. There are many sites that you can practice with paper money. Investopedia is a great site that gives you 100K in paper money, and you can either invest in the Canadian market or the US market. It even gives you the ability to use margin, which is a form of leverage since you are borrowing from your broker to invest more into your portfolio.

Now the screening part, how to find companies that

fit your criteria, well there many of them, but to simplify the process, we will concentrate on the ones that many follows. First, you must know how much profits are the company doing, and this can be good or bad. It depends on the sector of the business or the cycle of the business. Firm in their start will not have revenues or profits; one must have the ability to envision how big the company can become. Gains and dividends are usually at the later end of the cycle, it can be at its mature and stable cycle, and sometimes in its decline cycle.

Once we understand how profits and dividend operate, we must know what cycle we are looking to get in. Usually, companies that have a high price to earnings ratio indicate that the market expects a lot of growth. It does not mean that the markets are over evaluated; it says there is a lot of hype around the company. Netflix was an excellent example of high growth and P/E ratio in the hundreds.

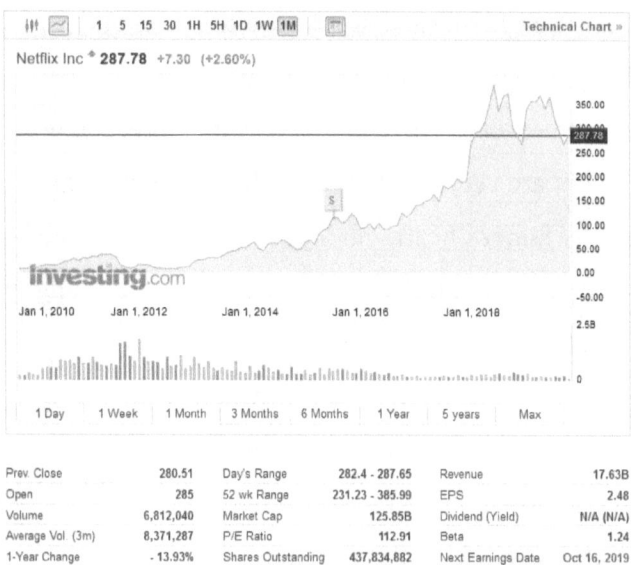

Even today, as we look at the company, it's still had a high P/E ratio. This company was called highly valued and that it should crash, well every year, it kept surprising us. For example, if you would have invested in 2012 10 000$, well today, you would be valued at 2 800 000$. We all have companies like this that we know.

The second criteria that we need to put in our screener, the size of the company. Also known as the market cap. I love companies that have a low cap but are very volatile. I would not recommend for the faint of heart, the bigger the company, the more stable returns that you will have. According to Investopedia;

· Small cap – 300 million to 2 billion
· Mid-cap – 2 billion to 10 billion
· Large-cap – 10 billion or more

How to find the capitalization of the company that you want to invest in, well it is straightforward, you multiply the number of shares in circulation by the price of the shares on the market. For example, a company has a million shares in circulation, and the price of each share is a 100$. Market = Number of Shares x Price = 1 000 000 x 10$/share = 10 000 000$, this would a be a very small company.

Now, these are very elemental criteria, but the point is to make this process simple for you to be able to execute quickly.

Now that we have some of our criteria, we need to look at our money management system, how much money is going to be invested in every trade, and how much are we going to allocate in all sector of the economy. According to a well-diversified portfolio, the portfolio must contain at least twenty stocks to eliminate non-systemic risk, the second aspect of the collection, the ponderation of the portfolio per sector of activity.

The best way to do the ponderation is to look at a benchmark that you will follow to compare your results of your portfolio, if you primarily invest in the US market, well a good reference would be the S&P 500.

- Information Technology – 19.9 percent
- Health Care – 15.8 percent
- Financials – 13.7 percent

- Consumer Discretionary – 9.9 percent
- Communications Services – 9.9 percent
- Industrials – 9.4 percent
- Consumer Staples – 7.4 percent
- Energy – 5.4 percent
- Utilities – 3.1 percent
- Real Estate – 2.9 percent
- Materials - 2.6 percent

Now we have a model that we can use to guide us to build our portfolio. What I recommend is take the time to find great companies before trying to invest in your money. If you can only see one great company, only buy that one and wait until you see the next great companies. What I have noticed is that the good companies I found in the past would outperform the market, but the companies that I had put in my portfolio to try to diversify would lose badly, which would bring down my performance.

Putting in the order, there are many ways an order can be placed, but I always put a limit order, this way, this ensure me that I won't overpay for the stock, if I put a limit of 1.5$ and the stock is trading at 1.49$, well the most I will pay, will be 1.5$, not placing a limit order can be disastrous in non-liquid market / stocks, some penny stock can explode in value when trying to buy them at the market value. It has happened to me, I bought a stock that was around 12 cents per share and I had accidentally put in at market, the stock went up to 26 cents a share, I got lucky since most of my dividends were bought at around 13 cents but then the problem was, I had a lot of profits on paper, but I could not sell my position for lack of liquidity.

Let's look at example, and we want to buy 10 000$ worth of apple, well the first thing that you need to do, is finding the ticker, the ticker is the abbreviation for the stock in the stock market.

The price of the stock is at 235$, so we take 10 000 / 235 = 42 shares, this means at the cost of 235$ we are able to buy 42 shares, then we need to preview the order, and if everything is correct in the it, you put in the offer and it might take a couple of minutes before the request gets completed. If you do not feel comfortable doing the order by yourselves, well, some brokers can help with the transaction.

Now, for more of a passive way to make some money, it's called buying an ETF that follows the market, buys an ETF that tracks the S&P 500 or the NASDAQ 100.

This chart shows how the **S&P** *500* has performed during the last 14 years, say you would have invested in 2009, 10 000$, today, the portfolio would be worth 29 693$, not bad, for a complete passive investment.

Now let's look at the **NASDAQ** 100.

10 000$ invested in 2009, well, that investment would be worth 78 600$. That is a fantastic investment. I believe that if one wants to be invested in the market, this is the way to go. What is also amazing about ETF is that they are almost no fees to them.

There are ways of trying to beat the market, but for a beginner, I would recommend following your economy, this is a sound investment, and it will give you the ability to live your life and being able to invest in the market without wasting so many hours trying to figure out, how to allocate your portfolio and spending a lot of time to see what strategy works.

Here are some sites that I use to get some information on the economy and stocks;

- Investing.com;
- Morningstar.com;
- Marketbeat.com;
- Marketwatch.com

I use investing.com to get the macro indicators of the US and world economy. I build my list of stocks that have the potential to explode to the upside, and this gives me the ability to follow them daily. I also the fed monitoring indicator to help me predict where are the interest rate are going. I try to either fix my mortgage rate if interest rates are going higher or use the variable rate if I think the market will go down. I have succeeded in some occasion, and wrong are some other instances. Trying to predict the market is a little like gambling.

Morningstar.com is used to get the SEC filling, annual reports, quarterly reports, and change in ownership of the company.

marketbeat.com gives me the ability to see who is buying the company, which institutions and funds are interested in the stock that I am following, I love to see a lot of ownership from institution since it is validating my research. Institution is also called smart money.

Source:

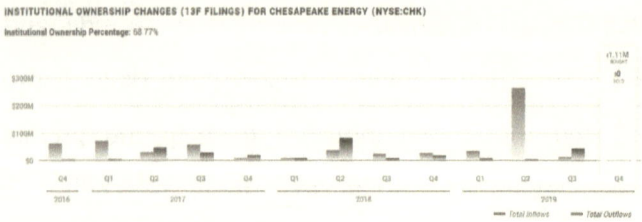

If more institution is buying, the probabilities of the price to increase will increase, since demand is higher than the offer.

Chesapeake Energy Stock Chart (NYSE:CHK)

They also have a robust charting system, and many technical indicators can be integrated, such as Bollinger bands and money flow indexes.

Note, there are some chances that markets could crash in the next years, but they could also keep increasing. In 2016, many great investors sold their position of the fact that they believed that the markets were going to crash. Well, now, in 2019, the market is still climbing. The best bet you can make is to allocate your portfolio in a way that you can favor a specific market in a particular cycle of the economy. Pondering your portfolio with some medium to long term bonds could be a great way to hedge your position against a fall of the markets.

Bonds tend to increase in value when interest falls; this increase in value can help with the losses made by the stocks of your portfolio. Therefore, the overall risk of the collection is always lower when bonds are integrated into your portfolio. Some people assume that is because the returns of the bonds are sure, well, that is right if the bond does not go insolvent, but the most significant factor to take into consideration is the fact that bonds fluctuate due to interest rate of the economy.

The bond must give the same interest as the market; this happens by price fluctuation and conveying the importance of the market.

Here are some necessary technical skills that can help to understand the direction of the market;

- Double bottom

- Head and shoulders

- Reverse head and shoulders

- Pennants

- Wedges

- Support and resistance area

Double bottom is shown by this pattern;

Double bottom helps to see reversals in the direction of the stock trend when prices have been falling for a long time, double bottom, if the breakthrough happens, will help to understand that the trend is perhaps going to go higher. Sometimes in a double bottom, we can see also a wedge starting to form. I love wedges, since, it is almost like pin pong, the momentum begins to increase since the ball is starting to accelerate and when it breaks through the upper line of the wedge it can explode to the upside.

The down wedges happen since there is a support to the bottom where the stocks hit multiple times, and the increase becomes smaller and smaller as time advances. If the stocks pass through the upper wedge, this stock could increase quickly.

Head and shoulders can be seen in this figure;

Head and shoulders can help to see when the stock has hit it's high and now could signal that the stock might start a reversal trend. Reversal head and shoulders are the same thing, but it indicates that the trend might reverse to the upside.

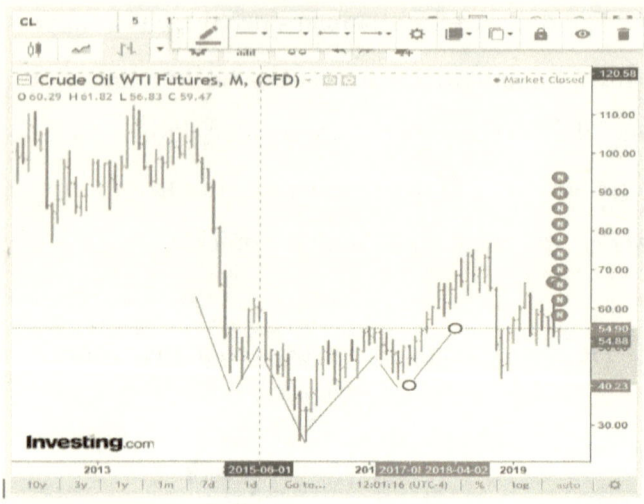

As we can, a reverse head and shoulders had happened with crude oil, starting in 2015 and finishing in 2017. When we were experiencing the decline of oil prices, I could begin to see the formation of the reverse head and shoulders, so I went all-in in oil stocks, which I was right, but my money management skills were not yet tuned to maximize my returns.

Pennants as flags happens, but they are rare, I seen this pattern once, and believe me when they arrive, you know that you are about to make some serious money.

When it happened, I made so much money in such a small amount of time that it made me sick at night. I could not believe that I was making all this money, and some people were not even able to eat three meals a day.

Support and resistance are easy to understand and see, support when it is pieced a resistance if the stock wants to go higher and vice versa. You can see supports at levels where the stock hit multiple time and then reverses. The same can be said in the other way when the stock hit the of the last highs. This becomes the resistance. Once it is pierced, the stock can rise quickly.

Macro indicators help to understand how the overall markets will react to the news; for example, if unemployment decreases, the stock market will tend to rise will the bond market will tend to lose value. Also, in the sense of crude oil prices, if inventory increases, well, the effect prices will tend to decrease since there is less demand than supply, always come back to the notion of the market equilibrium.

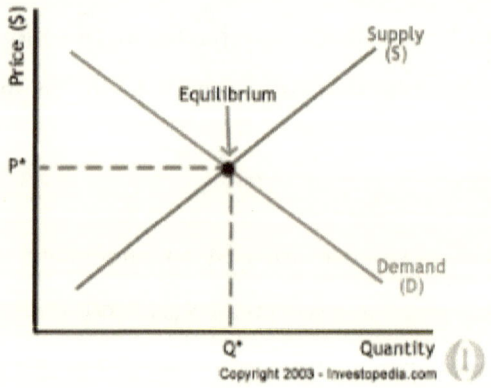

Copyright 2003 - Investopedia.com

This simple but practical help to determine the effect of supply and demand on price, if demand increases, we can expect that rates will increase, or vice versa. Now in the sense of amount, if supply increases, the price is expected to decrease. This is the same in demand for stocks, if demand increases for a stock, the price is expected to rise. Companies that buy back their share usually artificially increase the value of their capital; this is good for shareholders.

Investing in the market will help you to understand that what you believe to be accurate, is not close to the way reality works, many times you will think that you have a great idea of where the markets are going, but you will notice that most of the time, it goes the opposite way. Some might say that trading is secure, but I think this is the trap of the financial market, it lures you. I have heard from some brokers that they have clients that can beat the market year after year. These are the exception that study, buy and hold their stocks.

4 INTERNET INCOME

People are making money on the internet faster than ever before, and I see some guys get on YouTube, start from nothing and become millionaires in a couple of years. How I thought they were making their money was from their ads revenues, I could not grasp the concept of promoting products or services and how it worked.

Today I see all that potential, and if you are on Instagram, Facebook, and you have a big audience, you need to use them as clients. Everyone that follows you will buy what you wear or use. Have a beautiful watch on your wrist, well create an affiliate link to Amazon, and sell it. This process is fantastic, you do not need inventory or even need to start a business; all you need to do is promote.

Digital products can sell at a price, and the product has almost no cost to produce. The product can be shipped via E-mail; if the person does not like the product, well, he can be reimbursing. Digital books, audiobooks also fall in this category of income.

The form of income is usually royalties and licensing fees. You can also make some commission on products or services that you promote via affiliate marketing. There is clickbank.com that you can enroll for free.

There are many subjects that you can specialize in, here are a couple of examples;

- Arts & Entertainment Business/Investing
- Computers/Internet
- E-Business & E-Marketing
- Education
- Employment & Jobs
- Fiction
- Food, Wine & Cooking
- Games
- Green Products
- Health & Fitness

- Home & Garden
- Languages
- Mobile
- Parenting & Families
- Politics/Current Events
- Self Help
- Software & Services
- Spirituality, New Age & Alternative Beliefs
- Sports
- Travel

Once you have picked your niche, you will need to market your product for the demand of the market. It can be done by the title of your book or the keywords that you choose when inserting the keywords for people to find your product.

5 HAVE YOUR OWN PRINTING PRESS

Imagine that you could print money like the FED, many tell us about how banks can create wealth out of thin air, and the same can be said about the FED. Well, I had a friend that was furious about this process. His ideas got me thinking about how we the people could use a method that could simulate the same process.

I believe that real estate gives this ability, in the simple process of when the property gains in value, instead of selling the property and paying capital gains on the property, you refinance it, all the money that is deposited in your bank account is taxed free since the building has not been sold. Some might say, yes but you must pay it back, well it is true, but the tenants will repay the loan.

Now at first, this might not seem as if it is like having a printing press, but here how it gets interesting. The interest on that loan is usually close to inflation if your credit is excellent, plus you get to deduct the interest as an expense in the business.

Example refinance a property that went up twenty percent during the last five years. You bought the real estate deal for 200 000$, and you had 20% down payment on the deal, which means that you invested 40 thousand. The property is now worth 240 000$, and you refinance eighty percent of that amount. 240 000$ x 0.80 = 192 000. You had an original mortgage of 160 000$, you pay off the mortgage, and you are left with 32 000$.

32 000$ to invest in another deal or to cash out some

money. You get to deduct 192 000$ of interest to the income of the property. Say that the investment was of 3%, your tax of pay is about 50% and that inflation is at 2%.

5760$ can be applied to your expenses, thus reducing the taxes that you need to pay. It makes you save 50% of the fees. So, the cost of the interest has been divided by two.

5 760 * 0.5 = 2 880% cost interest minus taxes saved. It leads us to the last step, the real cast, after inflation. The inflation of 2% will decrease the value of the mortgage by 2%. 192 000 x 0.02 = 3 920$. The real cost after inflation on the loan will be of 2 880$ - 3 920$ = -1 040$. It means that you are being paid to take on debt. The inflation on the mortgage debt is higher than the cost of interest of the debt.

It is why I call this process the printing press.

ABOUT THE AUTHOR

I am a successful Real Estate investor - specializing in four units' properties. Investing in stock, outperforming the stock market in 2018. I have read many books on Self-development and spiritual workings.

Investing in tax liens certificates since 2013, many transactions were positively executed. I have help businesses focus their resources on doubling their income.

I've put into this book all the content that help me to become successful. The habits and secrets of the wealthy.